FOAL
Friends of the Arlington
Public Library

15

D0142101

E Y E S I G H T

What I Saw

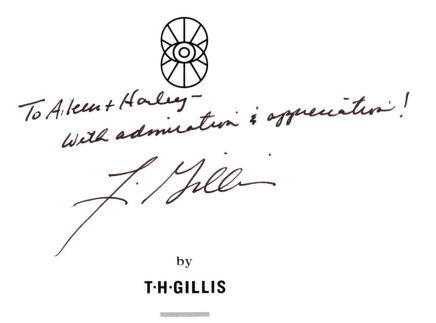

by

T·H·GILLIS

For Michelle

ISBN 978-0-578-79878-3

Table of Contents

CHAPTER TWO: REFLECTION 31

CHAPTER THREE: REFRACTION 51

CHAPTER FOUR: FOCUS 69

AFTERWORD: SUNSET 85

APPRECIATION 90

SUNRISE

On New Year's Day 2020, I announced my annual resolution on the social media site LinkedIn. It was simple and straightforward, and as I look back on it now—freeing. As I wrote it then,

> *"Here it is: To write one poem per week about something observed, without worrying about critics (real or imagined), including my own worst critic (myself)."*

I then committed to collect and publish the poems at the end of the year. As you might imagine, I made this promise openly as a way to seal the pledge—to myself. I earnestly wanted to see and know what would happen if I really could feel freed from judgment. It was an experiment.

The results are in. But first, a little context.

I've now been writing poetry for over a decade, and it took that full decade to complete my first book of poetry, entitled *Evensong: Prayers for Pilgrims*. Occupationally, I'm a lawyer, an accountant, a businessperson. I love things like competition and sports. To my regret— and yes, Mom always told me I would regret this—I cannot play a single musical instrument. With that resume, I am perhaps a most unlikely poet.

When I first started writing poetry, I thought of it as good, maybe even necessary, for me as a personal outlet. It was a form of private meditation, mindfulness or prayer. It was highly personal. I thought of my poetry as the amateur ramblings of a singular man who had experienced a little bit of life. Thus, I thought it was good for me, but not for others.

Deep down, though, I was worried about criticism—my own and others'.

In fact, had my friend Joe Dudeck not encouraged me to offer my poetry publicly, *Evensong* would not exist. But the words of a friend yielded my first release of my own tight-fisted grip about what I saw and felt and how I was evolving. And though the audience for any book of poetry is small (and for my book of poetry, infinitesimally smaller), the responses of *Evensong*'s readers were unexpected, heartfelt and so very positive and encouraging. Somehow, what I had recorded, resonated with others.

So, late in 2019, over the holidays, I wondered what would happen and how I would grow if I could be free of self-criticism and disbelief. What followed then from this New Year's resolution was unprecedented for me. I wrote 21 poems before the end of February; 51, between January 1 and April 30; and by the time Joe and Lindsay and Kiersten and Drew and I sat down to plot out this book, I had written nearly 100 poems during 2020. Not all of them will make this book, of course. I promised only one per week, or 52 for the year. I've added one extra poem at the end, an encore poem of sorts.

Of the 53 poems first published in this book, I wrote approximately ninety percent of them during 2020. Of the remaining ten percent, I revisited my own unpublished work from prior years and liked what I saw enough to include them herein. And the encore poem at the end is a special contribution from my daughter, Kiersten.

So the results are in. And, as it turns out, a judgment-free, no-fear zone can have a dramatic impact on personal creativity and productivity. In *The Artist's Way: A Spiritual Path to Higher Creativity*, Julia Cameron captured it this way:

> "*I learned to get out of the way and let the creative force work through me. I learned to just show up at the page and write down what I heard. Writing became more like eavesdropping and less like inventing a nuclear bomb . . . . I didn't have to be in the mood. I didn't have to take my emotional temperature to see if inspiration was pending. I simply wrote. No negotiations. Good? Bad? None of my business. I wasn't doing it. By resigning as the self-conscious author, I wrote freely.*"

I totally agree. And if nothing else emerges from the book you're now holding, I hope that the lesson I learned this year may somehow inspire you or someone else you know to live free.

❋ ❋ ❋   ❋ ❋ ❋   ❋ ❋ ❋

Chapter One

LIGHT

Every physical object in this vast universe, including our human bodies,
is built on the light of creation. Light beams became alive,
and became not only alive, but self-aware,
and acquired the ability to wonder.

The wonder is not whether this genesis
took six days or fourteen billion years or even eternity.

The wonder is that it happened.

—*Gerald Schroeder*

Even through your hardest days, remember we are all made of stardust.

—*Carl Sagan*

Open Up

Somewhere inside
There is an artist, latent
Waiting to be revived
In the heart, in the soul
Afraid to observe, much less depict
What lies within

The complication of that is
The beauty of the missed
Opportunity to behold
An unwritten story
A tale of courage and glory
That deserves to be told

Timeless

One day you will come to see
That this old photograph
Framed on the oaken credenza
Has a timeless quality

There we are so still and
Frozen in color tinged like sepia
Father, daughter, sons
Shades of blue, beige and grey

Permanence is lavender, indigo,
Magenta and smiles belie
The inner stresses that accompany
Early adulthood uncertainty

Yet amidst all that can distract
Our love is comforting and evident
And the color of forever is
Enduring, priceless, sempiternal

Full Flower

The beauty of love does not find its full flower
    In the young at heart
But in the old man and the old woman
    With weathered hands
Disembarking the southbound train
    Obviously ravaged by time and life

She with the stroke and he with the steady arm
    Extended to mind the gap
In the twilight they clasp one to another
    And patiently tread toward home
Astounded by all that has been
    Enamored by what's left to come

Thaumaturgical

Why should we think it all ends here
When it was always and ever
A miraculous presence here

This morning, the spindly legs
Of the spider in the loo
Decided it was time to move

And the cloud-blocked gaze
Of the sun in the space above
Chased away the gloom, the fog

But well before that all
I was drawn in by the thaumaturgical
And my eyes opened, I woke

Why should we think it all ends here
It was always and ever
A supernatural presence here

All I Do Not Know

On a morning like this
Why can't the world be silent
Why can't time stand still
To pay respects to the finite fragile

On a morning like this
When I look at my device
When I recall it is requisite
To life in the modern world

On a morning like this
Nothing is silent, nothing is quiet
Nothing I see even claws its way back
To soften the din and cacophony

On a morning like this
All I really want is to be still to know
All I really want is a sense of tomorrow
To comfort the mourners in loss and sorrow

On a morning like this
Thousands at risk with coronavirus
Millions of refugees with no place to live
And Kobe's family awakes to emptiness

On a morning like this
I confess aloud all I do not know
And I see Richard's early morning note
'You don't really need to know'

The Truth, When It Turns Out

The world was flat and then it wasn't
Turned out to be round all along
And the universe was geocentric
And then heliocentric
Until someone discovered
It was nothing of the centric sort
At all but rather peripheral
Or perhaps incommunicable
Or just not yet known

We once rode on a turtle's back,
And the center of the universe,
Some say, runs right through Tulsa
If only it were that simple

Now they say there is no center fix
Despite some gigantic scattermix
Out of apparently no where
And some indescribable no thing

Yet we still say the sun rises
When it really doesn't

So obvious now, these
Preconceived notions
And things we thought
Had to be true
But some of which
Weren't and aren't

[CONTINUED]

Concomitantly
Such a beautiful innocence
Can be attributed
To misunderstandings,
Myths, lies and prevarications,

Like the one I tell myself so often
(You know the one
You tell yourself, also)

That I am insufficient
When it turns out
I am enough

The Glory of Life

The glory of life is most evident
In the smallest of human events
Miniscule little moments
Of indescribable bliss

Like a newborn's first breath
And a wonder-wide smile
A toddler's first step
And that joyous first yell

For all who choose to see
Ordinary time as holy
The glory of life never disappears
Mid storm clouds or grotty air

It lasts into eternity
Like Mom's delightful ecstasy
When she tastes fresh fruit
And finds it sweet, sour or tart

One day I will yield and write
About something other
Than the mysterious nexus of
The sacred and secular

But the narrow ability
To articulate inexpressible beauty
Relentlessly intrigues me
To try and try and try again

Sparrows

Why sparrows when

From what I can see
They are the meanest in the aviary
Known as planet Earth

Prickly, nettlesome me-first

Petty little triflers
Who cheat and steal
Fight first, dine later

Dressed in drab, saddle-brown faded

Nothing much remarkable about that

When there are
Lovely and loving
Goldfinches and turtle doves
Woodpeckers and cardinals
And the merrily drunken catbird
A-wassailing on the fence

[CONTINUED]

They coexist like best friends
Teammates
And even feed the squirrels

Why sparrows

Sold five for two farthing
Or two for e'en less
Yet each one cherished

None unloved

If sparrows, then what . . .

Fear not

In full, this is
The Good News.

That Scarf I Hated

At the gate, I miss it

I'm fairly certain that my
short black scarf
is stuck in the security scanner
caught on its camera
over again and over

That scarf was so short
I hated it
until I lost it

It was still useful
I should have given it
to the homeless woman
in Tower Hill tunnel

She may have loved it

A Scene from Docklands Light Railway

She entered this world weightlessly
Held and carried, hugged and loved,
Now swung by her dad who found
A way to suspend a seat from two ropes
Between sky and ground, but all those
Attempts to fly alone and solo soar
Come crashing down into adulthood
And over many years, gravity has its way
Until one day the ground will prevail

Observation

The modern woman and
Contemporary man
So distracted
By breaking news

When all around are
Miracles
Both slow
And fast

What is essential
As it turns out
Is simply this:
Observation

springsign

and a gentle february rain
enticed the robins
to emerge from hiding
in winter's silence
to spring to life
in softened soil for
a protein morsel search

but one eschewed the worms
no doubt found in ground
in favor of the lofty perch
on the shivering river birch
from which she would sing
to celebrate
the signal flares of spring

Just This

Just this
Entrance into a new year
With a sky blue clear and crisp

Just this
Wonder and glory of the
Life I know I'll blink and miss

If I close my eyes to
Each moment since for
The moment itself is the resident bliss

[CONTINUED]

Just this
Everything I've ever known
Can be reduced to reminiscence

The auld lang syne
Celebration last night
Is now past and yields just this—

Gratitude for
Each moment now and
Each day thence

Just this

EYESIGHT

Chapter Two

REFLECTION

We cannot see our reflection in running water.
It is only in still water that we can see.

—*Zen Proverb*

Anything More Beautiful

Is there anything more beautiful than
The fresh green leaves of a sweet gum tree
Reimagined yellow by the fading light

Is there anything more lovely than
The sunburst yellow dress of a goldfinch
In flame on a branch in the morning light

Is there anything more compelling than
The enchanted amber of bee's knees
Presented in translucent glass on the kitchen table

Is there anything more regal than
The midsummer crown of a pieris floribunda
Awaiting cooler weather and inflorescence

Is there anything more stunning than
The magnificence of the flowering hibiscus
In the deadest heat of a sweltering summer

Is there anything more wondrous than
The slaphappy flight of the cabbage white
Butterfly crossing the garden, kite on string

Is there anything about this existence, this life
Received unwittingly as a splendid gift,
Is there anything about any of all of this—

That is not remarkable and glorious

Full Day, Small Snug

From the snug
I set out to
Watch a clock
Tick and tock
For one full day

In wonder, I did,
Wander, too,

And

After 34 minutes
I wanted something
More

Little Wren

Sing your lungs out, Little Wren
The world is alive and you,

You love community

Pandemic Lesson #1

This encounter is unlike any other
Unique and unprecedented
Long words beginning in U
Now forged together

From which there must be something to learn

The introduction of a novel virus
Hearkens to the Dark and Middle Ages
Long-lost words like famine and plague
Somehow we'd forgotten

There is nothing new under the sun, said Solomon

This coronavirus presents a new way to die
As if the world needed another
To supplement the myriad
Possibilities to ponder

Everyone is vulnerable, how fragile we are

So this morning, this hour, this solitary day
I pause for a few moments to consider
The pending and possible immediacy
Of my own mortality

It simply is what it is

[CONTINUED]

A conclusion that leads me to this—
That today is the compleat day
The absolute pinpoint moment
To say what I need to say

I love you so

For tomorrow I might be rendered
Incapacitated, speechless
Unable to let you know again
How very, very much

I love you so

So to you, my daughter,
And my three sons, too,
To all of you at once
And each one individually, too

To Jon and Zach and Kier and Drew
Please always remember, always know

I'm so very, very proud of you

The Energy of Interpersonal Electricity

I reached out for her hand
With my arm extended as far as I can
Til the tips of her fingers met up with mine
And interlaced a bit one more time
I closed my eyes and breathed a sigh
This is all I needed at this time

Ilex Verticellata & Opaca

The hilltop holly on Brawner
Is heavy and pregnant with the winterberries
Globose red drupe
Will ripen all winter
Until one day the garden will, with stir and frenzy,
Come alive to birds' delights

Why then and why not now?
The abundance is ready to be devoured
But the robins and mockingbirds
Thrashers and catbirds
Woodpeckers and bluebirds
Bluejays, cardinals,
Waxwings and mourning doves

Bide their time
Stalling their appetite
With winter's limited diet

[CONTINUED]

And then one day of one month
As if the appointment is destined
The American robins will gather and descend
As one to strip the bush tree bare
Lifting its load as I witnessed last year

Magnificent conflagration
Like a starling murmuration

Consider the birds, he said
They don't farm or work or store or save
But they feed alright,
Oh do they feed

If I could return to my twenties,
I hope I would remember
I hope I would remember to consider
The birds

Mostly Wait, But Sometimes Don't

For the most part
Waiting is a virtue

As in, during Advent,
Wait ————

with anticipation

Or in a joke,
Wait ————

Or in darkness,
hardship, adversity,

Hold on for the LIGHT!

❀ ❀ ❀   ❀ ❀ ❀   ❀ ❀ ❀

But exceptions apply, in which
Waiting is a vice

As in, with a deferred compliment
To a foe or to a friend,

Where waiting to say it may be a sin

[CONTINUED]

Or with a gift,
When the right day may never come again

Or at the end of a match,
With time running out,
And your failure to shoot
May prevent a win

* * *   * * *   * * *

But Wait ————

Isn't that life

The clock is ticking,
The trail may end
And the hard truth is
We never know when

The chance to do
Something good

Will end

Why I Sing

What if the universe is simply the breath of God
and the Big Bang the infinite moment when
she first put her lips around the bead of the balloon,
deeply inhaled and blew existence of all into life.
And what if the air I respire is the animation of God.
To be honest, I think this is why I sing.

Answered Prayer

I am so far removed
From what I want to be

Where I want to show love
    I show little regard
        for the thoughts and feelings of others

Where I want to be kind
    I condescend

Where I want to be gentle
    I lash out

Where I want to react
    in a way that demonstrates
        I am confident in the knowledge
            that I am beloved

Instead I react, out of
    insecurity and care for myself
        over the cares of others

Yes, I am a mess.
God, love me.
Please.

(written late 2006 or early 2007; rewritten, January 7, 2008; found, April 6, 2020; answered, somewhere between 2006 and 2020; possibly one of my first attempts at poetry as prayer; grateful for slow miracles)

What If

Even if true
Could a counterfeit twenty ever
Justify four armed officers
Three police cars
A face pinned on the ground
And a knee on a neck
For 8:46

No
No
No
Unquestionably and emphatically
No

Ten weeks into
Lockdown with forty million
Unemployed
Those who have must understand
What a pack of cigarettes
Is really worth—
Not this

What if
Store clerks had given them away
The proprietor had commended their grace
And banks had forgiven all debts
To the shareholders' applause and delight
And the officers had offered a hand
And simply helped George Floyd back to his home

Pandemic Lesson #2

between crises humans would build destroy and rebuild
entire economies macro and micro systems too big to
fail fossil-fueled streets and overcrowded cities arena
domes mass transit options suitable to accommodate
mass gatherings conferences concerts shows that must
go on and all of this far away from visibility of the gifts
of the universe —

good earth, warm light, pure air, fertile soil, abundant water,
fruited plants, shady trees, magnificent birds and animals
and fish and all they ever really needed —

and after this novel coronavirus they likely will again

unfathomable

i keep trying but can anyone
fathom any of this
from womb to tomb
from glint to grave

i have no idea
how I got here,
nor how here
was itself prepared

like nesting wombs

from mom's to earth's
and earth's to sun's
and sun's to galaxy's
and galaxy's to universe's
and universe's to ——

one womb, it seems,
gives birth to another
and somehow, some way
i am here

Wabi-Sabi

Perfection was never tied to Eden
Despite our preconceptions
How few hours or how few days
Passed til we consumed the tree

The beauty of everything
Resides in imperfection
The weathered look
The standing still to see

Driftwood from the sea
Now lies amid the dunes
Patina formed by way of storms
From origins unknown

The past will always
Be a simple fact of history
And not a final destiny
The end will justify the means

When the proper time comes
To take the perfectly
Symmetrical sweetgum tree
Tortured rings we'll see

[CONTINUED]

For all growth must
Endure the sculptor's cut
The lance, the spike
The bleed and bite

And the untended jungle
Is striking in its own way
As a well-manicured
English country garden

I know nothing truly perfect
Without practice, patience, suffering
But I can confidently prophesy
It's still what I will try to be—

(What a) Useless waste of energy.

Those who've gone and come again
Testify of love that always wins
That overcomes the arrogance
Of our self-loathing loneliness—

Love is the form of human kintsugi.

It's possible the earth was
Once fully covered by water

[CONTINUED]

Or perhaps like an asteroid,
Devoid of form and void

But mountains make majestic
Carved out by pressure forces
Exquisite and immense
Perfect by imperfection

And when a Carolina crescent moon
In the after-dusk sky
Illuminates the sidewinding palmetto
To call it disfigured, who am I?

Some have said we live in three's
Loneliness to solitude
On to hospitality
We discover our dependence

Others say it differently
Order to disorder
Then on to reorder
All is being made new

To me, it's wabi-sabi

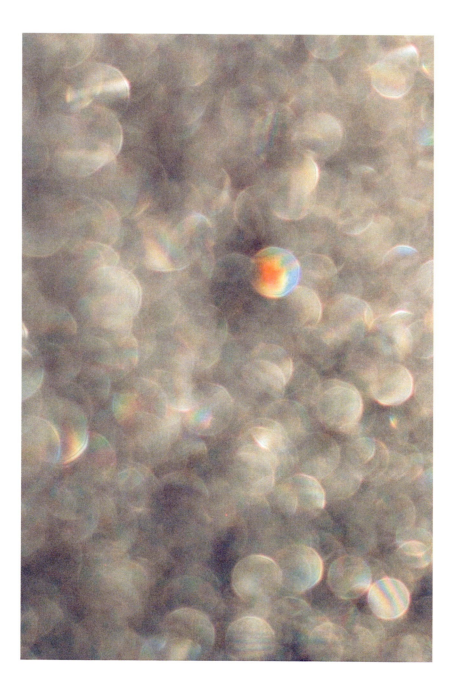

Chapter Three

REFRACTION

The colors of light are infinite through refraction, yet they all come from the same source. Thus, I cannot detach myself from the wickedest soul, nor fail to identify with the most virtuous.

—Dalai Lama

All I Need to Know

All I need to know
Is This, that I cannot control
Everything, that I am not alone
All I need to know Is This
The world on which I breathe is sun-kissed
It's been here, and I was made for this
All I need to know for this instant
All I need to know Is This—

I am dependent.

All I need to know
Is This, that I need not horde
Anything, for I am not alone
All I need to know Is This
Everything I need and I can coexist
As if I were made for this
All I need to know for this moment
All I need to know Is This—

I am derivative.

All I need to know
Is This, that my hand is held
Always, and even when I cannot feel
All I need to know Is This
The whisper in my ear is not careless
For I was made to hear Just This
All I need to know at this junction
All I need to know Is This—

I am loved.

Ideas of Heaven

The lovely young woman, the flexible yogi,
Lay on a soft blanket in a willowy garden
On her abdomen, feet to the gentle blue sky
Interrupted by a few breath-like wisps of clouds,
And with a graceful arch in her back and book in hand
She read from a thousand pages of historical fiction
While Finn rolled over on backscratch grass

One eye to this play yielded a sense of orlay
About which anyone might very well say
That. That. That is my idea of heaven.

And yet, she was bored,
As we all have been,
As we all were and are,
When the highway to productivity
Reroutes by pandemic detour

So here we all are
And there we all were
Without a sense of choice
Happy in some unison voice
Antsy to be on our way again

To what, we don't know

Perhaps heaven and hell may be one and the same
Is the absence of choice the very feature of hell
The scene in the garden in Kent did not tell

But in some strange and meaningful sense
It was both my idea of heaven and our idea of hell

[ ]

What I remember is the color of light
When reflected by a prism of delight
Onto the covered floor of the cabin

What I remember is the precision
When a plane pane of artificial glass
Transformed what was black and white

Into the most lustrous rainbow
I'd ever seen, just in front of me
On the spot where I'd just been

Truly, I thought, this is a holy place
A holy world, such a sacred space
I was born into this hallowed universe

Paupered and bedizened both
At the same time, I inhale the smoke
Nondual, exhilarating breath of God

Broadstairs

I stood on the sand in the surf among the white cliffs
Glistening on stage against a royal sapphire sky
And the floor-to-ceiling curtain of the refulgent wind
Shuttered my eyelids to make me sense it all in

Breath of the Spirit of God that it is
Made lift of dull arms and my weathered hands
And I floated with wings of fresh wisdom
Of connectedness with him

All this resplendence, this life-giving air
My crude comprehension, this magic that's here
All I see now and then, all I see everywhere
Is overwhelming, for these are broadstairs

Pieris Floribunda

Through the mountain fetterbush, andromeda
I think I see a kinglet, old world warbler,
And sometimes a cardinal, sparrow or wren
Silhouetted on a backdrop of a monk's hand

In focus on the foreground flowering pieris
A honeybee in suspense, upside down, drinks in
Nectar from foggy morning white fruit urns
That would be poisonous to anything else

Marvelous this moment to consider, to ponder
Saint Francis, pray for us in this moment of wonder

Sunflowers

I want to wake up and walk in a field full of sunflowers
with my mouth agape and laughing
at the unwitting joy
of the long-stem blossoming sunbeams

What color do you find the tip to be
other than cornflower
to attract a wandering honeybee
and the lovely young woman with a Birxian scarf

Jungfrau in a flower field all dressed in white
shimmers amidst the yellow tapestry
and makes it possible to remember
beauty in a time of woe

Rain in Two Acts

Act 1

Go to the woodland trust
Sit in the pouring rain
Watch the copper birch
Drink it in with gratitude

Act 2

Grace has been
A beautiful comfort in pain
On this parched heart,
My private desert,
Grace has felt like
Slow and gentle rain

Enemies

The more proximate the fire
The less need for dogma for
The flame does not burn but
Sheds more light
And exorcises fears of
Misunderstanding, of
Getting it wrong

Worry is the enemy of freedom
One enemy we need not love

Fear is the first sign of bondage
Peace unlocks the cell door

Birds-Eyes

Seagull

In a flash
One split second
When I had hardly turned my head
A slash of white
Yellow beak
Swooped in behind me
And took my sandwich,
My Earl,
A seagull —

Sixty miles from sea

I could only smile at her patience and ingenuity.

Pelicans

Prehistoric, pelicans find their prey
From a few hundred yards away
Every afternoon of every single day

And the unsuspecting fish
Becomes a proper dish
Long before it has a final wish

Head down, wings spread
Kamikaze, the predator descends
Gravity alone provides the wind

The dive a perfect ten
Sometimes loses, sometimes wins
The joy the chase, the fruit depends

Above Us Only Sky

In the center of frenzy

In the perverse way that life is most frenetic
Most kinetic
When human capacity is most severely limited
Most restricted

While this planet spins
At sixteen miles per minute
How is it we don't feel it

In the vise grip of complex midlife stresses
Midlife messes

It is really difficult to
Imagine

Pandemic Lesson #3

Puddleglum descended
Just before a raw Spring had begun.
The deep still of a moonless dark
Could be sensed at high noon
In the urban socially distanced park.
And all the addlepated
Knew it without a name
And never knew what happened,
Blindsided like Joe Theismann.

* * * * *

Pandemic and pandemonium
Share the same root for a reason

Day by saturnine day
Seventy-three or so it seemed
In one month alone just before May

Cases grew and deaths accumulated
Winds bit and skies mourned
To rationalize a plague's etymology

[CONTINUED]

And as the sun would settle
Underneath the horizon on
Another day without immunity

You'd wake the next day
Under the same pandemic spell
Of an unsympathetic insanity

Reminding of this mortality—
Even the myopic who contract this virus
Should still be prepared to go

* * * * *

From the simplicity of monotony
I watched as nature began
To rise, rise — to rise again

The sun emerged and found her voice,
And sang out to all of the trees
"Bring forth your leaves."

Each day, from bud to bloom
Samara to flower to leaf
Lungs of the earth expelled new verse

[CONTINUED]

* * * * *

All I ever may have sought
to achieve from the perfection ladder
Came to naught, exposed

As plans insufficient for the noble call
To receive the gifts of the earth
With gratitude and appreciation

For life, even in all
Its intrinsic insecurities, life itself
Is the most unnoticed miracle

Of all, and the largesse from this
Calamity is the reminder of
how fragile I am so

Slow down, sit awhile
Watch all living things grow
Spot Venus in the western afterglow

At the end of this sun salutation,
Clasp hands and bring thumbs to heart center
In this prayer, I'm still glad to be alive

Inequality

I cannot possibly understand your plight
You stand there in the intersection on the median divide
Between rows of cars staged to go at a traffic light
With a cardboard sign requesting some intervention
And your far-off gaze, the weathered countenance
The presence of numb and a heart of hopelessness

I wondered today where you must go at night
To spend the dark hours awaiting resurrection
I pondered what it must be like to live in the favela
Situated at the terminus end of the runway
The chance of life, the unfair conclusion
The way it is, defiance to long-known illusions

We must not leave it there

Thing He Really Said

He really said   *don't worry*

And applied it   *quite clearly*

Your life   *don't worry*
Your past   *don't worry*
Your future   *don't worry*
Your shelter   *don't worry*
Your clothing   *don't worry*
Your needs   *don't worry*
Your body   *don't worry*

Your yesterday   *don't worry*
Your tomorrow   *don't worry*

Of the birds and of the flowers   *see clearly*

It's that simple   *really*

Just watch

EYESIGHT

Chapter Four

FOCUS

God, whom we try to apprehend by the groping of our lives –
that self-same God is as pervasive and perceptible as the atmosphere
in which we are bathed. He encompasses us on all sides,
like the world itself.
So, what prevents you, then, from enfolding him in your arms?

Only one thing: your inability to see him.

—*Teilhard de Chardin, The Divine Milieu*

Yoga

We can be honest here

It's a whole lotta stretch

This work, this life

This toss and catch

Matter spins

And suffering

Sometimes wins

And threatens to

Stifle joy,

Asphyxiate.

But go with me

[CONTINUED]

To the beach at three

And watch the children

Play in the sea

They know nothing yet

Of the bitter tree

So light they are and

So carefree

The dexterity

Of a boy or girl

Barely past my knee

They're so unimpressed by gravity

ETA

the kingdom of God
is
within you

words of Jesus

who wants me

to believe
the gospel
good news that

time to destination

can be

0:00

Jigsaw

Shutterfly did it, and others will, too
My lovely young daughter, she asked them to
Take her photo and make it a jigsaw of
Our walk on the sand by the cliffs by the sea
With a peripatetic dog between you, between me

And with each little piece, I could not help but think
How did any of this here ever come to be?

For if I sat myself down and took out a pen
To write in a journal for the start of a plan
I would have no earthly idea how to begin to create
Anything in the world of which I populate

Not sand, not surf, not sky, not sun,
Not woman, not man, not even a hand
Not bird, not fish, not dog, not clam
Not color, not fog, not intricate function
Not air, not wind, not breath, not warmth
Not beauty, not life, not love, no none

I thought for awhile, and then awhile longer
The piece in my hand still another 'I couldn't'
So I went to sleep with these thoughts in my head
And woke to a world at the head of my bed
A wonderful world in which I am the blessed

Blessed are the observant,
For they shall see God
In a jigsaw puzzle
Of all places

Corona Coaster (One Possible Explanation)

And we all went back to work from home this morning
And sat in the same hard chairs hunched over qwerty boards
And fourteen-inch screens with images projected by zoom or teams
Thinking surely there is more to life than this

Nightly News

The sturgeon moon rose in the eastern sky wearing a blindfold
As if to avert the sight of Isaias' bead on the Carolina shoreline
And the sea rose to assault the land, meeting nonviolent resistance
This time, for the land received the bounty with joyous relief
From yet again another hottest summer on anyone's record
And for the fifth month in a row, the nightly news crew
Featured stories of pandemic cases and mask debates
And more inexplicable things the US president had said

If I were the moon, I'd close my eyes, too

Shekinah

Talk to me aloud
While I can still hear
And I will not react
As if surprised

for

I have long heard
You speak
Love into me from
Before I was three

and

The Shekinah
Light that you are
I know
From very deep within

The Loss of Gratitude

though the adage goes
'familiarity breeds contempt'
it is much much much
more sinister than that

like slow erosion

familiarity
rusts what's new
chips emotion
clips at wonder
denudes awe
into expectancy

what's lost in this
undesirable transformation
is knowledge of the true self
and the cosmic premise

so hampered by smog and light pollution

we forget
all of what we see and
all of what we know
is magical

and as the struggle
to be enthralled grows

so does unwarranted entitlement

and the loss of gratitude

As If Always

Falling star and wild thing

Forty minutes on the gritty shore

At low tide

Voice of wind

Din of wave

Taste of salt and

Breath of sand

Tactile reminders of my origins

And what I eat

And all I love

Were here from the

Beginning

Death, Maybe

Last night
I fell asleep in America
And woke up in another place
That still looked like home
Between then and now
Not exactly sure what happened
At least not in any specifics
I can corroborate
I closed my eyes
I slept
I woke
There I was

Is that
What death is like, I wondered,
To fall asleep on one side
And wake up on another
Where it feels just like the homeland
Not exactly sure what happens
At least not in any detail
That can be corroborated
I close my eyes
I sleep
I wake
There I am

Cottonwood Tree, Revisited

To those who live in a snow globe,
There is no past or future.
The moment is one present.
And the gentle wind, movement
Initiated by outside force.
An uncontrolled shake-'em up, of sorts.

Thus it was, one Sunday, one May,
With the drone and prehistoric sound
Of the early cicadas in the background,
The preemies, unexpected by years,
And the cottonwood on sixteen, the snowing tree
Releasing its clouds full of seeds.

We six stood, untrapped by the present,
But rather freed by life in that precise moment,
Neither regretting the losses or sins of our past
Or fearing the uncertain whims of the future.
In the now, we stood, awestruck by snow cotton
Drifting up and floating by—nature's miniature sky lanterns.

Brown Birds

Most of the birds I know are brown
    Sparrows and wrens, nuthatches and hens
They come by each early morning
    To show their gratitude
Though some will mistake that
    As a simple grab for food

But for me, they parade of course
    Lilting softly from perch to perch
On the feeders I stationed
    So I could join in their joy

I believe they are grateful
    I think they're full of joy
These birds, these lovely
    Simple brown yard birds

Yeah, they are sacred, too

All It Takes Is One

All it takes is One

One person, One ray of light
One observation, One spark of inspiration
One impression, One hint of dissatisfaction
One moment, One taste of awakening

All it takes is One

And it's rarely expected
And seldom announced,
But a seed of a thought,
Often planted by a stranger,
Somehow germinates
And changes everything

And for that you must be present

All it takes is One

Divine Milieu

In the end

When death comes and finally wins
It will arrive with no fanfare and no surprise
For all these fifty years and more
Like a firefly, I've long been drawn

To the light

In the peace of a moment
When I observe its warmth and comfort
Like a madeleine of somewhere
I feel like I know I've been before

From the heart

Conceived in passion and human love
Destined to unite again with
Whatever greater love lies behind
The beauty of earth and sky

In the flesh

Fresh from pondering incarnation
And the lessons of life's seasonal cycle
In confidence of some things eternal
I am now content to trust the light

In the end

When death comes and finally wins
It is only Pyrrhic in the end
For before my eyelids reach their rest
I will be absorbed into Love

EYESIGHT

SUNSET

For Christmas 2019, my oldest son, Jonathan, gave me a book of selected poems by William Carlos Williams, one of his favorite poets. Just last weekend (October 3-4, 2020), Danny Heitman, editor of Phi Kappa Phi's Forum magazine, wrote a column in the weekend review section of the Wall Street Journal on one of Williams' poems—a 16-word masterpiece entitled "The Red Wheelbarrow." In his retrospective, Heitman penned something wonderfully relevant to the book you are holding today. He wrote: "In a year when millions have been homebound by a pandemic, 'The Red Wheelbarrow' reminds us that we can gaze out our windows and find meaning, too—even if the view, at first glance, seems unremarkable."

What I aspired to do in 2020 was simply to write what I saw. What I saw often started as something that seemed unremarkable; but the more I reflected on what I saw, the more remarkable it became. Suddenly, it seemed that Teilhard de Chardin's divine milieu sprung to life for me. Reality is this: we live in a magical, supernatural world that feels so natural to us. We can try all we like, but adjectives to describe that paradox all seem to fail. And that is exactly what makes our existence, our universe, so mind-blowingly indescribable.

But we can try. And, as a simple layperson, I have tried to capture something of that attempt in these pages. I hope you'll try, too. Anyone can. We start so simply—with observation. What we see. And in all of this discovery during 2020, I found joy again, even in a pandemic year.

Finding joy was one of the great, unexpected benefits of the decade-long creation of my first book, *Evensong*; and that is why the first poem in *Evensong* was about just that—about finding joy. This is how that poem goes:

Where to Find Joy

In the very first breath of the day
In the slice of lemon perched on ice in a tumbler
In the magnificence of the Milky Way viewed from
Crested Butte, Mauna Kea or a dark jungle

In the 14 billion years of love expressed
In the universe since inception
In the pure expression of peace symbolized by a dove
In sunrise and sunset over the ocean

In the mystery that hides all I cannot know
In the rich fullness of the color spectrum

In the diverse ways streams and rivers flow
In the comforting warmth of the midday sun

In the gentle eyes and gaze of a woman
In the tell-tale markings on a whale's tail
In the breathtaking vistas on top of Table Mountain
In the manner in which penguins mate

In the fin of a 14-foot great white shark
In the exquisite design of the flowering protea
In the unexpected escape to be found in Central Park
In the birth of a child and the death of a saint

Ah, joy
Elusive and yet obvious
Hidden but evident
Accessible any moment of any God-given day
In everybody, everything, and everywhere

This is where to find joy

* * *   * * *   * * *

A highlight of 2020 was when my daughter, Kiersten, wrote me from Edinburgh during the pandemic. "Dear Dad," she wrote,

> "Watching Evensong Episode 2 (a video-recorded reading of Where to Find Joy, which you can find at thgillis.us) inspired me to search for the joy in my own life. I often get caught up in the stress of work and forget to acknowledge the simple joys that are always there. Thank you for sharing your thoughts and inspiring change in others. Here's the raw version of my jotted down joys of life. I thought you may enjoy it. Love always, Kieraboo."

Here's what she wrote during 2020, too:

Where to Find Joy
by Kiersten Gillis

In the rich smell of early morning coffee
In the mystical nature of a low fog
In the heartfelt embrace with a dog
In the perfectly golden color of toast
In a plant that thrives under your care
In the expectant face of a horse waiting for grain
In a warm smile from a friend
In the monogamous love between ducks
In a sudden and powerful thunderstorm
In the green, green color of grass
In the memories brought back by an old song
In a long phone call with a mother, father or brother
In the sparkling of a cleaned kitchen
In the incredible view from the top of a mountain
In the loving squeeze from a parent
In the first buds of spring
In the first snow of winter

✳ ✳ ✳   ✳ ✳ ✳   ✳ ✳ ✳

Ah, joy
Elusive and yet obvious
Hidden but evident
Accessible any moment of any God-given day
In everybody, everything, and everywhere

This is where to find joy

A SPECIAL NOTE REGARDING 2020

Finally, a word about this unusual year of 2020. This book was planned and announced before we knew about a new contagion that would sweep the planet and before issues of racial injustice and social inequity began receiving the front-page treatment they so rightly deserve.

This book is not a book of pandemic poetry. It is also not a treatise on racial injustice or social equity. Yet these issues are part of what I observed; therefore, I have listened and thought and written some about them during the year. What I present in the form of any poetry on these topics is presented with humility, for I write only from one person's perspective.

I do want any readers to know that I observed these things and that I want to understand and participate in the process of uniting heaven and earth. As the prayer that Jesus taught us to pray goes, "Your kingdom come, your will be done, on earth as it is in heaven."

Nevertheless, as my perspective is so limited, I would ask the reader to forgive me for anything I have written that is foolish. In short, I ask for your grace in those moments where my artistic side has tried to process witnessed suffering and injustice.

I'll never run for political office, so I don't need any votes; but I am quite human—I do desire love. So, if I've said something in poetry that offends, please love me and let me know. Help me learn.

APPRECIATION

A book is no solitary venture, at least not in my case. I love the community that forms around the process of publication.

Thank you, Michelle, for loving and encouraging me to pursue my wild-eyed, fanciful dreams and ideas. I love you!

Thank you, Joe Dudeck, for your initial prodding to produce *Evensong* in 2017 and for encouraging me to think more boldly as I head toward retirement. Thanks also for your great photographs and your willingness to go at this one more time! You can find Joe at his website: joetography.us.

Thank you, Lindsay Dudeck and Kiersten Gillis, for your poem selections, reviews and edits. This is the hard work of these projects. I'm so grateful!

Thank you, Drew Gillis, for your role with your friends in creating music inspired by this book. It will be great to have on my new website: thgillis.us.

Thank you, Stacey and Jon McClure of Co-motion, for your work on branding and layout. I love the new brand. You can find Stacey and Jon at their website: comotion.studio.

Thank you, Jon and Zach Gillis, for inspiring me to stay creative and energized in my late 50s.

Thank you, David Leo Schultz. When I watch your passion and fire for the arts and your never-say-never attitude, it makes me want to create more. Your direction and production of three full feature-length movies about Rich Mullins, Brennan Manning and St. Francis, respectively, on shoe-string budgets, still amazes me. You can see them at watch.ragamuffintv.com or other streaming services. Thanks for shooting my *Evensong* videos, too.

Thank you, Bobby Polito and the Metro 29 Band of Brothers—too many to list, but you know who you are—you revived me.

Thank you, Barbara Pyles, for teaching me both the joy of English Literature & Composition from 1978-81 and the confidence that I could write, too.

Thank you, readers of *Evensong*, because your responses inspired me to do this project.

* * *   * * *   * * *